Eʰ alto saxoph...

essential
Musicianship
for band
ensemble
concepts

Eddie Green
John Benzer
David Bertman

ISBN 978-0-634-08843-8

HAL•LEONARD®
CORPORATION
7777 W. BLUEMOUND RD. P.O. BOX 13819 MILWAUKEE, WI 53213

1. Establishing Sound

1–1 Block Concert F

 ### Student Goals
1. Breathe together.
2. Start together.
3. Follow through with the same air and **vowel sound**.
4. Release together.
5. **Organize** the end of each note as clearly as the beginning.
6. Vibrato-producing instruments can alternately play a straight tone or with vibrato.

1–2 Concert F – Non-Touching Notes

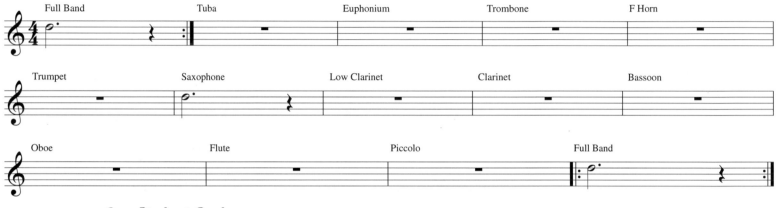

 ### Student Goals
1. Breathe together.
2. Start together.
3. **Match tonal energy (strength, resonance, characteristic sound)**.
4. Match articulation.
5. Release together.
6. Match **pitch** level from section to section, whether in unison or octaves.
7. Vibrato-producing instruments can alternately play a straight tone or with vibrato.
8. The resonance and **body of sound** should be equal from instrument to instrument and from octave to octave.
9. During whole rests, breathe on count 3.

1–3 Concert F – Touching Notes

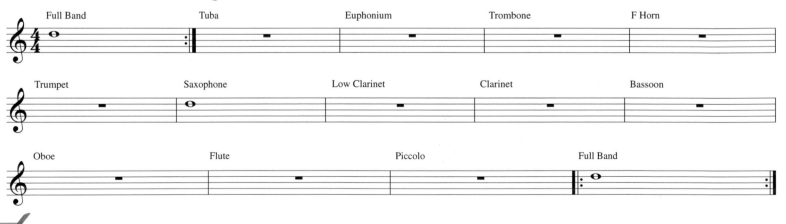

Student Goals
1. Breathe together.
2. Start together.
3. **Match tonal energy.**
4. Match articulation.
5. Pay particular attention to the air at the end of each note to connect it smoothly with those that follow.
6. At the end of the exercise, the release should sound as **organized** and clean as the articulation at the beginning.
7. Vibrato-producing instruments can alternately play a straight tone or with vibrato.
8. The **resonance** and **body of sound** should be equal from instrument to instrument and from octave to octave.
9. During whole rests, breathe on count 3.

Boldface words are terms that can be found in the glossary at the back of the book.

1–4 Color Drill

 Student Goals

1. Breathe together.
2. Start together.
3. Follow through with the same air and **vowel sound**.
4. Release together.
5. **Organize** the end of each note as clearly as the beginning.
6. Vibrato-producing instruments can alternately play a straight tone or with vibrato.
7. **Match pitch** level from section to section, whether in unison or octaves.

8. The **resonance** and **body of sound** should be equal from instrument to instrument and from octave to octave.
9. Pay particular attention to the air at the end of each note to connect it smoothly with those that follow.
10. Woodwinds naturally create a more **vibrant** sound than brass. The brass should match the naturally vibrant sound of the woodwinds.
11. Breathe on count 3 before entrances.

2. Establishing Articulation

2–1 Articulation Drill – Long To Short Note Values

 Student Goals

1. Breathe together.
2. Start together.
3. **Match tonal energy**.
4. Match articulation.
5. Release together.
6. Match **pitch** level from section to section, whether in unison or octaves.
7. Posture should be natural. The body position should be balanced with the ribcage up and shoulders sloped.
8. When taking a breath, feel cool air move over the tongue. This air should continue to the diaphragm area below the rib cage.
9. The face should feel natural, and the texture of the lips should be soft.
10. Palms and elbows should feel soft and relaxed.

11. The tongue should move up and down naturally, not back and forth (Conductor will explain and give tasks).
12. The same part of the tongue goes to the same spot with the same **strength** every time.
13. The tongue should return to its natural position during rests ("**musical silence**").
14. As notes get quicker, more air should be moved down the center of the mouthpiece/instrument.
15. Articulation should not weaken as rhythms become more active.
16. The embouchure should never move during rests.
17. The body should not move during rests.
18. As the metronome produces new subdivisions, they should be "**internalized**".
19. During whole rests, breathe on count 3.

Boldface words are terms that can be found in the glossary at the back of the book.

2–2 Articulation Drill – Short to Long Note Values

 Student Goals

1. Breathe together.
2. Start together.
3. **Match tonal energy**.
4. Match articulation.
5. Release together.
6. Match **pitch** level from section to section, whether in unison or octaves.
7. Posture should be natural. The body position should be balanced with the ribcage up and shoulders sloped.
8. When taking a breath, feel cool air move over the tongue. This air should continue to the diaphragm area below the rib cage.
9. The face should feel natural, and the texture of the lips should be soft.
10. Palms and elbows should feel soft and relaxed.
11. The tongue should move up and down naturally, not back and forth (Conductor will explain and give tasks).
12. The same part of the tongue goes to the same spot with the same **strength** every time.
13. The tongue should return to its natural position during rests ("**musical silence**").
14. Keep the air stream centered as rhythms become less active.
15. Articulation should not weaken as rhythms become more active.
16. The embouchure should never move during rests.
17. The body should not move during rests.
18. As the metronome produces new subdivisions, they should be "**internalized**".
19. During whole rests, breathe on count 3.

2–3 Articulation Drill – Long to Short Note Values

 Student Goals

1. Breathe together.
2. Start together.
3. **Match tonal energy**.
4. Match articulation.
5. Release together.
6. Match **pitch** level from section to section, whether in unison or octaves.
7. Posture should be natural. The body position should be balanced with the ribcage up and shoulders sloped.
8. When taking a breath, feel cool air move over the tongue. This air should continue to the diaphragm area below the rib cage
9. The face should feel natural, and the texture of the lips should be soft.
10. Palms and elbows should feel soft and relaxed.
11. The tongue should move up and down naturally, not back and forth (Conductor will explain and give tasks).
12. The same part of the tongue goes to the same spot with the same **strength** every time.
13. The tongue should return to its natural position during rests ("**musical silence**").
14. As notes get quicker, more air should be moved down the center of the mouthpiece/instrument.
15. Articulation should not weaken as rhythms become more active.
16. The embouchure should never move during rests.
17. The body should not move during rests.
18. Until this drill is mastered, breathe on count 4 of any measure before air is needed.

2–4 Articulation Control Exercise – Long to Short Note Values

 Student Goals

1. Breathe together.
2. Start together.
3. **Match tonal energy**.
4. Match articulation.
5. Release together.
6. Match **pitch** level from section to section, whether in unison or octaves.
7. Posture should be natural. The body position should be balanced with the ribcage up and shoulders sloped.
8. When taking a breath, feel cool air move over the tongue. This air should continue to the diaphragm area below the rib cage.
9. The face should feel natural, and the texture of the lips should be soft.

10. Palms and elbows should feel soft and relaxed.
11. The tongue should move up and down naturally, not back and forth (Conductor will explain and give tasks).
12. The same part of the tongue goes to the same spot with the same **strength** every time.
13. The tongue should return to its natural position during rests ("**musical silence**").
14. As notes get quicker, more air should be moved down the center of the mouthpiece/instrument.
15. Articulation should not weaken as rhythms become more active.
16. The embouchure should never move during rests.
17. The body should not move during rests.
18. Breathe on count 4 quarter rests.

2–5 Articulation Control Exercise – Short to Long Note Values

 Student Goals Refer to 2–4

2–6 Pick-Up Note Drill #1 (Ascending)

 Student Goals

1. All pick-up notes should have the same **tonal energy** as the note following them.
2. Articulation on all pick-up notes should **match**.
3. Each pick-up note should have forward motion toward the downbeat. The exception to this rule is when the downbeat note is a higher pitch than the pick-up note(s). This is further clarified in Student Goal #5.

4. All pick-up notes should be the same note length.
5. Downbeat notes that are higher **pitches** than the pick-up note should not sound stronger than the pick-up note.
6. Breathe on each count 2.
• Include all aspects of sound organization in exercise 1.

2–7 Pick-Up Note Drill #2 (Ascending)

Student Goals Refer to 2–6

2–8 Pick-Up Note Drill #3 (Ascending)

 Student Goals Refer to 2–6

2–9 Pick-Up Note Drill #1 (Descending)

 Student Goals Refer to 2–6

2–10 Pick-Up Note Drill #2 (Descending)

 Student Goals Refer to 2–6

2–11 Pick-Up Note Drill #3 (Descending)

 Student Goals Refer to 2–6

3. Linear Intervals Up and Down

3–1 Descending Intervals Created Up and Down

 Student Goals

1. Breathe together.
2. Start together.
3. Follow through with the same air and **vowel sound**.
4. Release together.
5. **Organize** the end of each note as clearly as the beginning.
6. Strive for a clear tone quality without extraneous noises.

7. The middle note of each group should **match** the surrounding notes in sound and volume.
8. The third note of each group should match the **tonal energy** and **pitch** center of the first note.
9. The wider the interval, the more focused the air stream should be.

10. It is the woodwinds' responsibility to produce accurate intervals to support the brass.
11. As intervals expand, it is important the tonal **resonance** remains consistent from note to note - and instrument to instrument (i.e., the half step and the fifth should match).
12. Breathe on count 4 quarter rests.

3–2 Ascending Intervals

 Student Goals

1. Breathe together.
2. Start together.
3. Follow through with the same air and **vowel sound**.
4. Release together.
5. **Organize** the end of each note as clearly as the beginning.
6. Strive for a clear tone quality without extraneous noises.
7. The middle note of each group should **match** the surrounding notes in sound and volume.

8. The third note of each group should match the **tonal energy** and **pitch** center of the first note.
9. The wider the interval, the more focused the air stream should be.
10. It is the woodwinds' responsibility to produce accurate intervals to support the brass.
11. As intervals expand, it is important the tonal **resonance** remains consistent from note to note - and instrument to instrument (i.e., the half step and the fifth should match).

12. As intervals expand, the middle note should not have a **"thinner"** tone quality.
13. As intervals expand, reach lower in the body for air.
14. As intervals expand, the lips should remain soft and natural - the corners provide **strength** to support air direction for brass players.
15. Breathe on count 4 quarter rests.

Boldface words are terms that can be found in the glossary at the back of the book.

4. Vertical Intervals Created Up and Down

4–1 Expanding Interval Flow Drill

 Student Goals

1. Breathe together.
2. Start together.
3. Follow through with the same air and **vowel sound**.
4. Release together.
5. **Organize** the end of each note as clearly as the beginning.
6. Strive for a clear tone quality without extraneous noises.
7. The middle note of each group should **match** the surrounding notes in sound and volume.
8. The third note of each group should match the **tonal energy** and **pitch** center of the first note.
9. The wider the interval, the more focused the air stream should be.
10. It is the woodwinds' responsibility to produce accurate intervals to support the brass.

11. As intervals expand, it is important the tonal **resonance** remains consistent from note to note - and instrument to instrument (i.e., the half step and the fifth should match).
12. As intervals expand, the middle note should not have a "**thinner**" tone quality.
13. As intervals expand, reach lower in the body for air.
14. As intervals expand, the lips should remain soft and natural - the corners provide **strength** to support air direction for brass players.
15. It is more difficult to match expanding intervals. The player should intensify the air stream to support the wider interval.
16. The **resonance** of sound should relate to the first note.
17. At the end, play the tritone interval with confidence.
18. Breathe on count 4 quarter rests.

4–2 Expanding Interval Flow Drill – Non-Touching Notes (Model and Ensemble)

 Student Goals

1. Breathe together.
2. **Match tonal energy**.
3. Match articulation.
4. Release together.
5. Match **pitch** level from section to section, whether in unison or octaves.
6. Posture should be natural. The body position should be balanced with the ribcage up and shoulders sloped.

7. When taking a breath, feel cool air move over the tongue. This air should continue to the diaphragm area below the rib cage.
8. The face should be natural, and the texture of the lips should be soft.
9. Palms and elbows should feel soft and relaxed.
10. In order for eighth notes to have the same **tonal strength** as longer note values, the air should get to the **back of the note** sooner.
11. Breathe on count 4 quarter rests.

Boldface words are terms that can be found in the glossary at the back of the book.

4–3 Expanding Interval Flow Drill – Touching Notes (Model and Ensemble)

 Student Goals

1. Breathe together.
2. **Match tonal energy**.
3. Match articulation.
4. Pay particular attention to the air at the end of each note to connect it smoothly with those that follow.
5. At the end of the exercise, the release should sound as **organized** and clean as the articulation at the beginning.
6. Release together.
7. Match **pitch** level from section to section, whether in unison or octaves.
8. Posture should be natural. The body position should be balanced with the ribcage up and shoulders sloped.

9. When taking a breath, feel cool air move over the tongue. This air should continue to the diaphragm area below the rib cage.
10. The face should be natural, and the texture of the lips should be soft.
11. Palms and elbows should feel soft and relaxed.
12. Because eighth notes have shorter durations, the air should get to the **back of the note** sooner.
13. The wider the interval, the more focused the air stream should be.
14. At the end, play the tritone interval with confidence.
15. Breathe on count 4 quarter rests.

4–4 Parallel Interval Flow Drill – Touching Half Notes (Model and Ensemble)

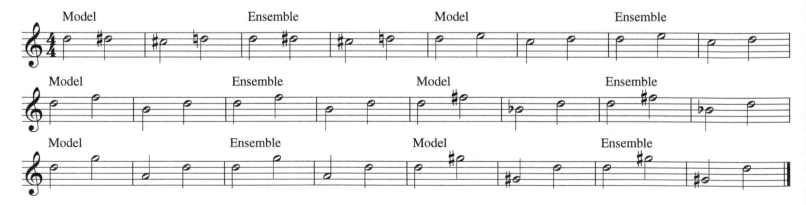

 Student Goals

1. Breathe together.
2. Start together.
3. Follow through with the same air and **vowel sound**.
4. Release together.
5. **Organize** the end of each note as clearly as the beginning.
6. Strive for a clear tone quality without extraneous noises.

7. The middle note of each group should **match** the surrounding notes in sound and volume.
8. The third note of each group should match the **tonal energy** and **pitch** center of the first note.
9. The wider the interval, the more focused the air stream should be.
10. Breathe on count 3 before entrances.
    cont.

Student Goals

11. As intervals expand, it is important the tonal **resonance** remains consistent from note to note - and instrument to instrument (i.e., the half step and the fifth should **match**).
12. As intervals expand, the middle note should not have a "**thinner**" tone quality.
13. As intervals expand, reach lower in the body for air.
14. As intervals expand, the lips should remain soft and natural - the corners provide **strength** and air direction.
15. The **model** and ensemble notes should touch each other.
16. The consistency of air should remain the same from note to note.
17. The tonal resonance of the model and ensemble should match.
18. The movement of the ensemble should be as clear as the model.
19. At the end, play the tritone interval with confidence.

4–5 Parallel Interval Flow Drill – Non-Touching Notes (Model and Ensemble)

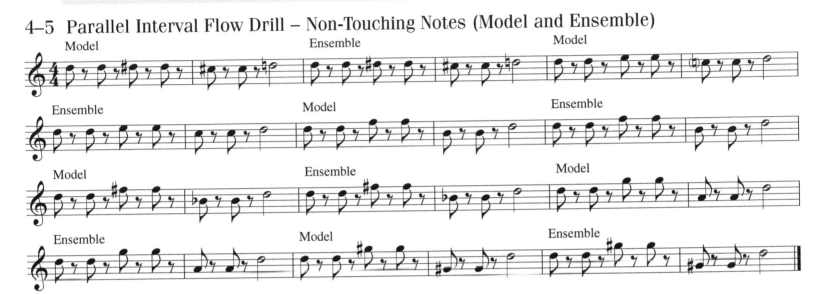

 Student Goals

1. Breathe together.
2. **Match tonal energy**.
3. Match articulation.
4. Release together.
5. Match the **pitch** level between sections and specific instruments (i.e., trombone to horn).
6. Posture should be natural. The body position should be balanced with the ribcage up and shoulders sloped.
7. When taking a breath, feel cool air move over the tongue. This air should continue to the diaphragm area below the rib cage.
8. The face should be natural, and the texture of the lips should be soft.
9. Palms and elbows should feel soft and relaxed.
10. Because eighth notes have shorter durations, the air should get to the **back of the note** sooner.
11. The ensemble should sound as clear as the **model**.
12. Breathe on count 3 before entrances.
13. At the end, play the tritone interval with confidence.

4–6 Parallel Interval Flow Drill – Touching Quarter Notes (Model and Ensemble)

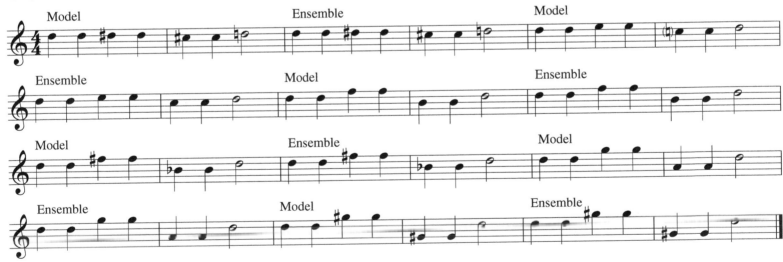

 Student Goals

1. Breathe together.
2. **Match tonal energy**.
3. Match articulation.
4. Release together.
5. Match the **pitch** level between sections and specific instruments (i.e., trombone to horn).
6. Posture should be natural. The body position should be balanced with the ribcage up and shoulders sloped.
7. When taking a breath, feel cool air move over the tongue. This air should continue to the diaphragm area below the rib cage.
8. The face should be natural, and the texture of the lips should be soft.
9. Palms and elbows should feel soft and relaxed.
10. The ensemble should sound as clear as the **model**.
11. At the end, play the tritone interval with confidence.

5. Note Lengths

5–1 Ascending Combined Skill Drill – Non-Touching Notes (Model and Ensemble)

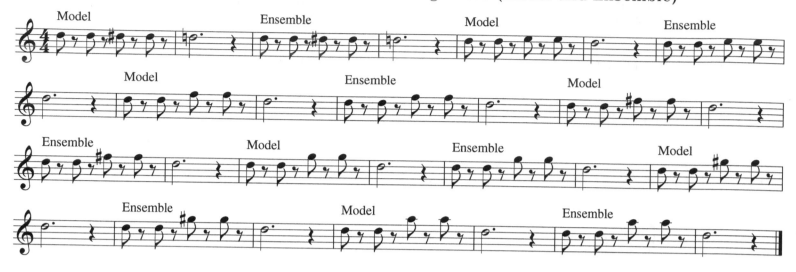

 Student Goals

1. Breathe together.
2. Start together.
3. **Match tonal energy**.
4. Match articulation.
5. Release together.
6. Match **pitch** level from section to section, whether in unison or octaves.
7. Posture should be natural. The body position balanced with the ribcage up and shoulders sloped. The body and face should remain still.
8. When taking a breath, feel cool air move over the tongue. This air should continue to the diaphragm area below the rib cage.
9. The face should be natural, and lip texture should be soft.
10. The ensemble should sound as clear as the **model**.
11. Palms and elbows should feel soft and relaxed.
12. Because eighth notes have shorter durations, the air should get to the **back of the note** sooner.
13. Breathe on count 4 quarter rests.

5–2 Descending Combined Drill – Non-Touching Notes

 Student Goals

1. Breathe together.
2. **Match tonal energy**.
3. Match articulation.
4. Release together.
5. Match **pitch** level from section to section, whether in unison or octaves.
6. Posture should be natural. The body position should be balanced with the ribcage up and shoulders sloped.
7. When taking a breath, feel cool air move over the tongue. This air should continue to the diaphragm area below the rib cage.
8. The face should be natural, and the texture of the lips should be soft.
9. Palms and elbows should feel soft and relaxed.
10. Because eighth notes have shorter durations, the air should get to the **back of the note** sooner.
11. The ensemble should sound as clear as the **model**.
12. Breathe on count 4 quarter rests.

Boldface words are terms that can be found in the glossary at the back of the book.

5–3 Ascending Combined Skill Drill – Touching Notes (Model and Ensemble)

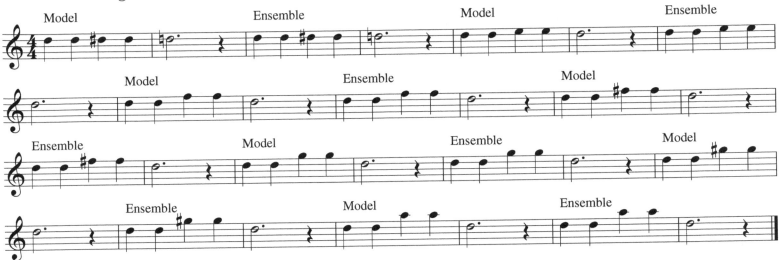

 ### Student Goals

1. Breathe together.
2. **Match tonal energy**.
3. Match articulation.
4. Pay particular attention to the air at the end of each note to connect it smoothly with those that follow.
5. At the end of the exercise, the release should sound as **organized** and clean as the articulation at the beginning.
6. Release together.
7. Match **pitch** level from section to section, whether in unison or octaves.
8. Posture should be natural. The body position should be balanced with the ribcage up and shoulders sloped.
9. Feel cool air moving over the tongue and below the ribcage when taking a breath.
10. The face should be natural, and the texture of the lips should be soft.
11. Palms and elbows should feel soft and relaxed.
12. The ensemble should sound as clear as the **model**.
13. Breathe on count 4 quarter rests.

5–4 Descending Combined Skill Drill – Touching Notes (Model and Ensemble)

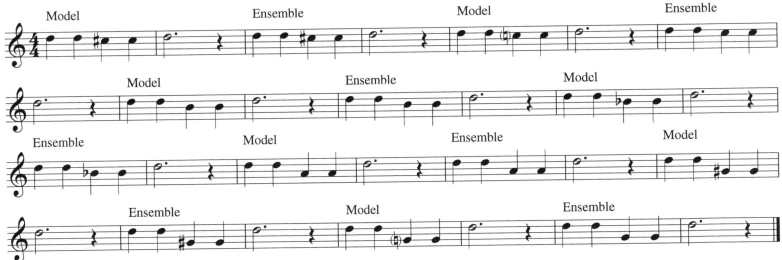

 ### Student Goals

1. Breathe together.
2. **Match tonal energy**.
3. Match articulation.
4. Release together.
5. Match **pitch** level from section to section, whether in unison or octaves.
6. Posture should be natural. The body position should be balanced with the ribcage up and shoulders sloped.
7. When taking a breath, feel cool air move over the tongue. This air should continue to the diaphragm area below the rib cage.
8. The face should be natural, and the texture of the lips should be soft.
9. Palms and elbows should feel soft and relaxed.
10. Because eighth notes have shorter durations, the air should get to the **back of the note** sooner.
11. The wider the interval, the more **resonant** the lower note should be.
12. The ensemble should sound as clear as the **model**.
13. Breathe on count 4 quarter rests.

5–5 Style Exercise – Perfect Fifths/Long to Short Note Values

 Student Goals

1. Breathe together.
2. Start together.
3. **Match tonal energy**.
4. Match articulation.
5. Release together.
6. Match **pitch** level from section to section, whether in unison or octaves.
7. Posture should be natural. The body position should be balanced with the ribcage up and shoulders sloped.
8. Feel cool air moving over the tongue and below the ribcage when taking a breath.
9. The face should feel natural, and the texture of the lips should be .
10. Palms and elbows should feel and relaxed.

11. The tongue should move up and down naturally, not back and forth (Conductor will explain and give tasks).
12. The same part of the tongue goes to the same spot with the same **strength** every time.
13. The tongue should return to its natural position during rests ("**musical silence**").
14. As notes get quicker, more air should be moved down the center of the mouthpiece/instrument.
15. Articulation should not weaken as rhythms become more active.
16. The embouchure should never move during rests.
17. Breathe on count 4 quarter rests.
18. All parts are interchangeable, but should remain in **balance** throughout the exercise.

5–6 Style Exercise – Perfect Fifths/Non-Changing Notes

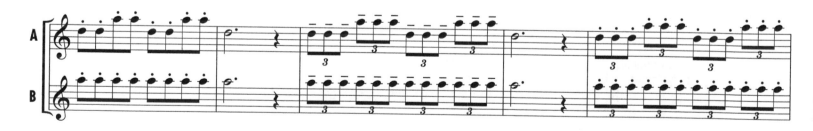

 Student Goals

1. Breathe together.
2. Start together.
3. **Match tonal energy**.
4. Match articulation.
5. Release together.
6. Match **pitch** level from section to section, whether in unison or octaves.
7. Posture should be natural. The body position should be balanced with the ribcage up and shoulders sloped.
8. Feel cool air moving over the tongue and below the ribcage when taking a breath.
9. The face should feel natural, and the texture of the lips should be soft. *cont.*

Student Goals

10. Palms and elbows should feel soft and relaxed.
11. The tongue should move up and down naturally, not back and forth (Conductor will explain and give tasks).
12. The same part of the tongue goes to the same spot with the same **strength** every time.
13. The tongue should return to its natural position during rests ("**musical silence**").
14. As notes get quicker, more air should be moved down the center of the mouthpiece/instrument.

15. Articulation should not weaken as rhythms become more active.
16. The embouchure should never move during rests.
17. Breathe on count 4 quarter rests.
18. All parts are interchangeable, but should remain in **balance** throughout the exercise.
19. As **pitches** ascend, the higher note should not be louder than the lower note.
20. As pitches descend, the lower note should not be softer than the higher note.

5–7 Style Exercise – Perfect Fourths/Non-Changing Notes

 Student Goals Refer to 5–6

5–8 Style Exercise – Major Thirds/Non-Changing Notes

 Student Goals Refer to 5–6

5–9 Style Exercise – Minor Thirds/Non-Changing Notes

 ### Student Goals

1. Breathe together.
2. Start together.
3. **Match tonal energy**.
4. Match articulation.
5. Release together.
6. Match **pitch** level from section to section, whether in unison or octaves.
7. Posture should be natural. The body position should be balanced with the ribcage up and shoulders sloped.
8. Feel cool air moving over the tongue and below the ribcage when taking a breath.
9. The face should feel natural, and the texture of the lips should be soft.
10. Palms and elbows should feel soft and relaxed.
11. The tongue should move up and down naturally, not back and forth (Conductor will explain and give tasks).

12. The same part of the tongue goes to the same spot with the same **strength** every time.
13. The tongue should return to its natural position during rests ("**musical silence**").
14. As notes get quicker, more air should be moved down the center of the mouthpiece/instrument.
15. Articulation should not weaken as rhythms become more active.
16. The embouchure should never move during rests.
17. Breathe on count 4 quarter rests.
18. All parts are interchangeable, but should remain in **balance** throughout the exercise.
19. As **pitches** ascend, the higher note should not be louder than the lower note.
20. As pitches descend, the lower note should not be softer than the higher note.

5–10 Style Exercise – Major Seconds/Non-Changing Notes

Student Goals Refer to 5–9

5–11 Style Exercise – Perfect Fifths/Non-Changing Notes

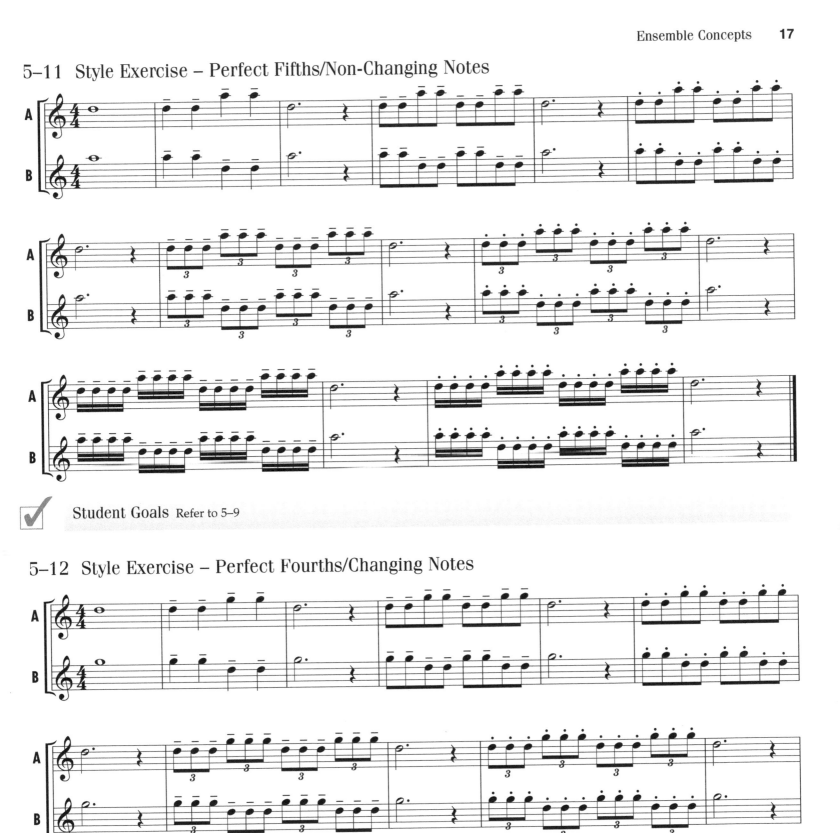

✔ **Student Goals** Refer to 5–9

5–12 Style Exercise – Perfect Fourths/Changing Notes

 Student Goals Refer to 5–9

5–13 Style Exercise – Major Thirds/Changing Notes

 Student Goals

1. Breathe together.
2. Start together.
3. **Match tonal energy**.
4. Match articulation.
5. Release together.
6. Match **pitch** level from section to section, whether in unison or octaves.
7. Posture should be natural. The body position should be balanced with the ribcage up and shoulders sloped.
8. Feel cool air moving over the tongue and below the ribcage when taking a breath.
9. The face should feel natural, and the texture of the lips should be soft.
10. Palms and elbows should feel soft and relaxed.
11. The tongue should move up and down naturally, not back and forth (Conductor will explain and give tasks).
12. The same part of the tongue goes to the same spot with the same **strength** every time.
13. The tongue should return to its natural position during rests ("**musical silence**").
14. As notes get quicker, more air should be moved down the center of the mouthpiece/instrument.
15. Articulation should not weaken as rhythms become more active.
16. The embouchure should never move during rests.
17. Breathe on count 4 quarter rests.
18. All parts are interchangeable, but should remain in **balance** throughout the exercise.
19. As **pitches** ascend, the higher note should not be louder than the lower note.
20. As pitches descend, the lower note should not be softer than the higher note.

5–14 Style Exercise – Minor Thirds/Changing Notes

Student Goals Refer to 5–13

5–15 Style Exercise – Major Seconds/Changing Notes

Student Goals Refer to 5–13

6. Creating Intervals with a Pedal Tone

6–1 Ascending Intervals With Pedal Tone

 Common Student Goals
1. Breathe together.
2. Start together.
3. Follow through with the same air and **vowel sound**.
4. Release together.
5. **Organize** the end of each note as clearly as the beginning.

Student Goals for Line A
1. Strive for a clear tone quality without extraneous noises.
2. The middle note of each group should not have a different sound or volume than the notes on either side.
3. The third note of each group should **match** the **tonal energy** and **pitch** center of the first note.
4. The wider the interval, the more focused the air stream should be.
5. It is the woodwinds' responsibility to produce accurate intervals to support the brass.
6. As intervals expand, it is important the tonal **resonance** remains consistent from note to note -
   and instrument to instrument (i.e., the half step and the fifth should match).
7. As intervals expand, the middle note should not have a "**thinner**" tone quality.
8. As intervals expand, reach lower in the body for air.
9. As intervals expand, the lips should remain soft and natural - the corners provide **strength** to support air direction for brass players.
10. Breathe on count 4 quarter rests.

Student Goals for Line B
1. Vibrato-producing instruments can alternately play a straight tone or with vibrato.
2. Take a breath before one is needed, then re-enter discreetly with the same volume and tonal resonance.

Boldface words are terms that can be found in the glossary at the back of the book.

6–2 Descending Intervals With Pedal Tone

 Student Goals Refer to 6–1

6–3 Parallel Intervals With Pedal Tone

 Student Goals for Line A
1. **Match** the **tonal energy** and **resonance** from note to note.
2. Avoid **"bumps" moving from note to note** by keeping the air constant between notes.
3. Be sure the fingers and tongue move exactly together.
4. **Energize** the air from note to note, especially larger intervals, however, do not let the air speed slow down as the intervals decrease.
5. Do not change the air speed between intervals (the **vowel sound** may change in the brass).
6. Play through the note between the concert Fs.
7. Breathe on count 4 quarter rests.

Student Goals for Line B
1. Vibrato-producing instruments can alternately play a straight tone or with vibrato.
2. Take a breath before one is needed, then re-enter discreetly with the same volume and tonal resonance.

6–4 Interval Pass-through

 Student Goals for Line A
1. The director will introduce the principle of **line movement**. Be sure to understand the concepts involved.
2. The **resonance** of each interval should **match** the resonance in line B.
3. As the rhythmic durations become shorter the interval needs "lock" quicker.
4. Regardless of the rhythmic structure, the air should continue through the end of the line.
5. At the beginning of this exercise, the second note leads the line forward and functions as part of the cadence, so it should lead strongly from the first note but be equal to the third note. Do the same for measures 3 - 4 and 5 - 6.
6. Breathe on count 4 quarter rests.
7. Gradually increase the amount of measures played in one breath.

Student Goals for Line B
1. Breathe together.
2. Start together.
3. Follow through with the same air and **vowel sound**.
4. Release together.
5. **Organize** the end of each note as clearly as the beginning.
6. Vibrato-producing instruments can alternately play a straight tone or with vibrato.
7. Take a breath before one is needed, then re-enter discreetly with the same volume and tonal resonance.
8. Strive to play the entire exercise in one breath.

6-5 Combined Perfect Fifths With Pedal Tone

 Student Goals

1. Breathe together.
2. Start together.
3. **Match tonal energy**.
4. Match articulation.
5. Release together.
6. Match **pitch** level from section to section, whether in unison or octaves.
7. Posture should be natural. The body position should be balanced with the ribcage up and shoulders sloped.
8. Feel cool air moving over the tongue and below the ribcage when taking a breath.
9. The face should feel natural, and the texture of the lips should be soft.
10. Palms and elbows should feel soft and relaxed.
11. The tongue should move up and down naturally, not back and forth (Conductor will explain and give tasks).

12. The same part of the tongue goes to the same spot with the same **strength** every time.
13. The tongue should return to its natural position during rests ("**musical silence**").
14. As notes get quicker, more air should be moved down the center of the mouthpiece/instrument.
15. Articulation should not weaken as rhythms become more active.
16. The embouchure should never move during rests.
17. Breathe on count 4 quarter rests.
18. All parts are interchangeable, but should remain in **balance** throughout the exercise.
19. As **pitches** ascend, the higher note should not be louder than the lower note.
20. As pitches descend, the lower note should not be softer than the higher note.
21. Those playing the **pedal tone** should exaggerate the strength of their articulation when compared to those changing pitches.

6-6 Combined Perfect Fourths With Pedal Tone

Student Goals Refer to 6–5

6–7 Combined Major Thirds With Pedal Tone

 Student Goals Refer to 6–5

6–8 Combined Minor Thirds With Pedal Tone

 Student Goals Refer to 6–5

6–9 Combined Major Seconds With Pedal Tone

 Student Goals

1. Breathe together.
2. Start together.
3. **Match tonal energy**.
4. Match articulation.
5. Release together.
6. Match **pitch** level from section to section, whether in unison or octaves.
7. Posture should be natural. The body position should be balanced with the ribcage up and shoulders sloped.
8. Feel cool air moving over the tongue and below the ribcage when taking a breath.
9. The face should feel natural, and the texture of the lips should be soft.
10. Palms and elbows should feel soft and relaxed.
11. The tongue should move up and down naturally, not back and forth (Conductor will explain and give tasks).
12. The same part of the tongue goes to the same spot with the same **strength** every time.
13. The tongue should return to its natural position during rests ("**musical silence**").
14. As notes get quicker, more air should be moved down the center of the mouthpiece/instrument.
15. Articulation should not weaken as rhythms become more active.
16. The embouchure should never move during rests.
17. Breathe on count 4 quarter rests.
18. All parts are interchangeable, but should remain in **balance** throughout the exercise.
19. As **pitches** ascend, the higher note should not be louder than the lower note.
20. As pitches descend, the lower note should not be softer than the higher note.
21. Those playing the **pedal tone** should exaggerate the strength of their articulation when compared to those changing pitches.
22. Do not back away from whole step dissonances.

6–10 Combined Minor Seconds With Pedal Tone

 Student Goals Refer to 6–9

6–11 Small to Large Descending Intervals With Pedal Tone

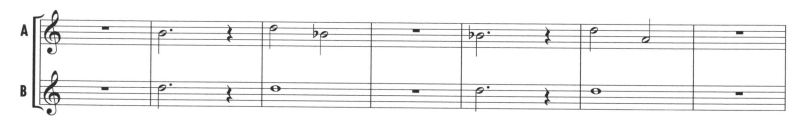

Common Student Goals

1. Breathe together.
2. Start together.
3. Follow through with the same air and **vowel sound**.
4. Release together.
5. **Organize** the end of each note as clearly as the beginning.
6. **Balance** between parts should stay the same.
7. Each interval **resonance** should be as clear as each unison resonance.

Student Goals for Line A

1. Strive for a clear tone quality without extraneous noises.
2. The second note of each group should have the same **tonal energy** and **pitch** center as the first note.
3. All parts are interchangeable, but should remain in balance throughout the exercise.
4. The wider the interval, the more focused the air stream should be.
5. It is the woodwinds' responsibility to produce accurate intervals to support the brass.
6. As intervals expand, it is important the tonal resonance remains consistent from note to note - and instrument to instrument (i.e., the half step and the fifth should **match**).

Student Goals for Line B

1. Vibrato-producing instruments can alternately play a straight tone or with vibrato.
2. Breathe on count 3 during whole rests and on count 4 quarter rests.

6–12 Small to Large Ascending Intervals With Pedal Tone

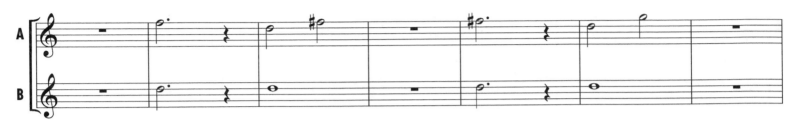

Common Student Goals

1. Breathe together.
2. Start together.
3. Follow through with the same air and **vowel sound**.
4. Release together.
5. **Organize** the end of each note as clearly as the beginning.
6. **Balance** between parts should stay the same.
7. Each interval **resonance** should be as clear as each unison resonance.

Student Goals for Line A

1. Strive for a clear tone quality without extraneous noises.
2. The second note of each group should have the same **tonal energy** and **pitch** center as the first note.
3. All parts are interchangeable, but should remain in balance throughout the exercise.
4. The wider the interval, the more focused the air stream should be.
5. It is the woodwinds' responsibility to produce accurate intervals to support the brass.
6. As intervals expand, it is important the tonal resonance remains consistent from note to note - and instrument to instrument (i.e., the half step and the fifth should **match**).

Student Goals for Line B

1. Vibrato-producing instruments can alternately play a straight tone or with vibrato.
2. Breathe on count 3 during whole rests and on count 4 quarter rests.

6–13   Small to Large Descending Intervals With Pedal Tone

Common Student Goals

1. Breathe together.
2. Start together.
3. Follow through with the same air and **vowel sound**.
4. Release together.
5. **Organize** the end of each note as clearly as the beginning.
6. **Balance** between parts should stay the same.
7. Each interval **resonance** should be as clear as each unison resonance.
8. The first and last unison should sound the same.

Student Goals for Line A

1. Strive for a clear tone quality without extraneous noises.
2. The second note of each group should have the same **tonal energy** and **pitch** center as the first note.
3. All parts are interchangeable, but should remain in balance throughout the exercise.
4. The wider the interval, the more focused the air stream should be.
5. It is the woodwinds' responsibility to produce accurate intervals to support the brass.
6. As intervals expand, it is important the tonal resonance remains consistent from note to note - and instrument to instrument (i.e., the half step and the fifth should **match**).

Student Goals for Line B

1. Vibrato-producing instruments can alternately play a straight tone or with vibrato.
2. Breathe on count 3 during whole rests and on count 4 quarter rests.

6–14 Small to Large Ascending Intervals With Pedal Tone

 ### Common Student Goals

1. Breathe together.
2. Start together.
3. Follow through with the same air and **vowel sound**.
4. Release together.
5. **Organize** the end of each note as clearly as the beginning.
6. **Balance** between parts should stay the same.
7. Each interval **resonance** should be as clear as each unison resonance.
8. The first and last unison should sound the same.

 ### Student Goals for Line A

1. Strive for a clear tone quality without extraneous noises.
2. The second note of each group should have the same **tonal energy** and **pitch** center as the first note.
3. All parts are interchangeable, but should remain in balance throughout the exercise.
4. The wider the interval, the more focused the air stream should be.
5. It is the woodwinds' responsibility to produce accurate intervals to support the brass.
6. As intervals expand, it is important the tonal resonance remains consistent from note to note - and instrument to instrument (i.e., the half step and the fifth should **match**).

 ### Student Goals for Line B

1. Vibrato-producing instruments can alternately play a straight tone or with vibrato.
2. Breathe on count 3 during whole rests and on count 4 quarter rests.

7. Extending Skills in Lower Register

7–1 Descending Concert F Scale (Two-Note Segments)

 ### Student Goals

1. Breathe together.
2. Start together.
3. Follow through with the same air and **vowel sound**.
4. Release together.
5. Pay particular attention to the air at the end of each note to connect it smoothly with those that follow.
6. The fingers and tongue should move together.
7. **Match tonal energy** as the **pitches** descend.

8. **Organize** he ends of the notes before rests as clearly as the beginnings.
9. The second note of any two-note pattern should be the same volume as the first.
10. Listen to make sure the **balance** of the ensemble remains constant throughout the exercise.
11. Tone quality should not change character from note to note.
12. Breathe on count 3 before entrances.

Boldface words are terms that can be found in the glossary at the back of the book.

7–2 Descending Concert F Scale – WW Model/Brass Lip Vibrations (Four and Eight-Note Segments)

* Silently finger/position cued notes while remaining in correct playing position.

 ### Student Goals Refer to 7–1

7–3 Descending Concert F Scale – WW Model (Triple Rhythms)/Brass Half Notes (Four and Eight-Note Segments)

* Silently finger/position cued notes while remaining in correct playing position.

 ### Student Goals Refer to 7–1

7–4 Complete Descending Concert F Scale – WW Model/Brass Lip Vibrations (Two-Note Segments)

* Silently finger/position cued notes while
remaining in correct playing position.

 Student Goals

1. Breathe together.
2. Start together.
3. Follow through with the same air and **vowel sound**.
4. Release together.
5. Pay particular attention to the air at the end of each note to connect it smoothly with those that follow.
6. The fingers and tongue should move together.
7. **Match tonal energy** as the **pitches** descend.
8. **Organize** the ends of the notes before "**silent fingerings**" as clearly as the beginning of the next note you actually play.

9. The second note of any two-note pattern should not be louder of er that the first - this applies to the eighth-note patterns as well.
10. Listen to make sure the **balance** of the ensemble remains constant throughout the exercise.
11. Tone quality can not change character from note to note.
12. All woodwind releases should touch the brass entrances, and vice versa.
13. Breathe on count 3 before entrances.

7–5 Complete Descending Concert F Scale – WW Model (Duple Rhythms)/Brass Half Notes (Two-Note Segments)

* Silently finger/position cued notes while
remaining in correct playing position.

 Student Goals

1. Breathe together.
2. Start together.
3. Follow through with the same air and **vowel sound**.
4. Release together.
5. Pay particular attention to the air at the end of each note to connect it smoothly with those that follow.
6. The fingers and tongue should move together.
7. **Match tonal energy** as the **pitches** descend.
8. **Organize** the ends of the notes before "**silent fingerings**" as clearly as the beginning of the next note you actually play.

9. The second note of any two-note pattern should not be louder of er that the first - this applies to the eighth-note patterns as well.
10. Listen to make sure the **balance** of the ensemble remains constant throughout the exercise.
11. Tone quality can not change character from note to note.
12. All woodwind releases should touch the brass entrances, and vice versa.
13. The woodwind articulation and **tonal strength** should not weaken as the exercise develops.
14. Breathe on count 3 before entrances.

8. Extending Skills in Upper Register

8–1 Ascending Concert F Scale (Two-Note Segments)

 Student Goals
1. Breathe together.
2. Start together.
3. Follow through with the same air and **vowel sound**.
4. Release together.
5. Pay particular attention to the air at the end of each note to connect it smoothly with those that follow.
6. The fingers and tongue should move together.
7. **Match tonal energy** as the **pitches** descend.
8. **Organize** the end of each note as clearly as the beginning.
9. The second note of any two-note pattern should be the same volume as the first.
10. Listen to make sure the **balance** of the ensemble remains constant throughout the exercise.
11. Tone quality should not change character from note to note.
12. Breathe on count 3 before entrances.

8–2 Ascending Concert F Scale – WW Model/Brass Lip Vibrations (Four and Eight-Note Segments)

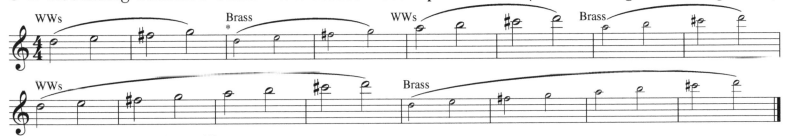

* Silently finger/position cued notes while remaining in correct playing position.

 Student Goals
1. Breathe together.
2. Start together.
3. Follow through with the same air and **vowel sound**.
4. Release together.
5. Pay particular attention to the air at the end of each note to connect it smoothly with those that follow.
6. The fingers and tongue should move together.
7. **Match tonal energy** as the **pitches** ascend.
8. **Organize** the ends of the notes before "silent fingerings" as clearly as the beginning of the next note you actually play.
9. Listen to make sure the **balance** of the ensemble remains constant throughout the exercise.
10. Tone quality should not change character from note to note.
11. All woodwind releases should touch the brass entrances, and vice versa.
12. Breathe on count 3 before entrances.

8–3 Ascending Concert F Scale – WW Model (Triple Rhythms)/Brass on Instruments (Four and Eight-Note Segments)

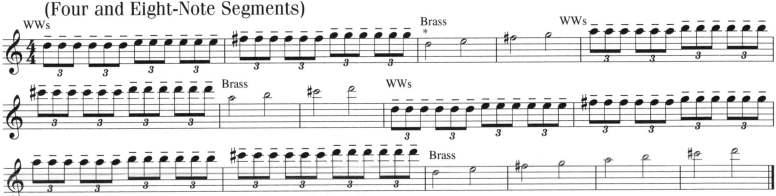

* Silently finger/position cued notes while remaining in correct playing position.

 Student Goals
1. Breathe together.
2. Start together.
3. Follow through with the same air and **vowel sound**.
4. Release together.
5. Pay particular attention to the air at the end of each note to connect it smoothly with those that follow.
6. The fingers and tongue should move together.
7. **Match tonal energy** as the **pitches** ascend.
8. **Organize** the ends of the notes before "**silent fingerings**" as clearly as the beginning of the next note you actually play.
9 . Listen to make sure the **balance** of the ensemble remains constant throughout the exercise.
10. Tone quality should not change character from note to note.
11. All woodwind releases should touch the brass entrances, and vice versa.
12. The woodwind articulation and **tonal strength** should not weaken as the exercise develops.
13. Breathe on count 3 before entrances.

Boldface words are terms that can be found in the glossary at the back of the book.

8–4 Complete Ascending Concert F Scale – WW Model/Brass Lip Vibrations (Two-Note Segments)

* Silently finger/position cued notes while
  remaining in correct playing position.

 ### Student Goals

1. Breathe together.
2. Start together.
3. Follow through with the same air and **vowel sound**.
4. Release together.
5. Pay particular attention to the air at the end of each note to connect it smoothly with those that follow.
6. The fingers and tongue should move together.
7. **Match tonal energy** as the **pitches** descend.
8. **Organize** the ends of the notes before **"silent fingerings"** as clearly as the beginning of the next note you actually play.

9. The second note of any two-note pattern should not be louder or softer than the first - this applies to the eighth-note patterns as well.
10. Listen to make sure the **balance** of the ensemble remains constant throughout the exercise.
11. Tone quality should not change character from note to note.
12. All woodwind releases should touch the brass entrances, and vice versa.
13. Breathe on count 3 before entrances.

8–5 Complete Ascending Concert F Scale – WW Model (Duple Rhythms)/Brass Half Notes

* Silently finger/position cued notes while
  remaining in correct playing position.

 ### Student Goals

1. Breathe together.
2. Start together.
3. Follow through with the same air and **vowel sound**.
4. Release together.
5. Pay particular attention to the air at the end of each note to connect it smoothly with those that follow.
6. The fingers and tongue should move together.
7. **Match tonal energy** as the **pitches** descend.
8. **Organize** the ends of the notes before **"silent fingerings"** as clearly as the beginning of the next note you actually play.

9. The second note of any two-note pattern should not be louder or softer than the first - this applies to the eighth-note patterns as well.
10. Listen to make sure the **balance** of the ensemble remains constant throughout the exercise.
11. Tone quality can not change character from note to note.
12. All woodwind releases should touch the brass entrances, and vice versa.
13. The woodwind articulation and **tonal strength** should not weaken as the exercise develops.
14. Breathe on count 3 before entrances.

9. Combining Elements

9–1 Ascending/Descending Parallel Intervals

 Student Goals

1. Breathe together.
2. Start together.
3. Follow through with the same air and **vowel sound**.
4. Release together.
5. **Organize** the end of each note as clearly as the beginning.
6. **Match tonal energy** and **resonance** from note to note.
7. Avoid **"bumps" moving from note to note** by keeping the air constant between notes.
8. Be sure the fingers and tongue move exactly together.
9. **Energize** the air from note to note, especially larger intervals, however, do not let the air speed slow down as the intervals decrease.
10. Do not change the air speed between intervals (the vowel sound may change in the brass).
11. Play through the note between the concert Fs.
12. Breathe on count 4 quarter rests.

9–2 Combined Ascending/Descending Intervals

 Student Goals

1. Breathe together.
2. Start together.
3. Follow through with the same air and **vowel sound**.
4. Release together.
5. **Organize** the end of each note as clearly as the beginning.
6. Strive for a clear tone quality without extraneous noises.
7. The middle note of each group should **match** the surrounding notes in sound and volume.
8. The third note of each group should match the **tonal energy** and **pitch** center of the first note.
9. The wider the interval, the more focused the air stream should be.
10. It is the woodwinds' responsibility to produce accurate intervals to support the brass.
11. As intervals expand, it is important the tonal **resonance** remains consistent from note to note - and instrument to instrument (i.e., the half step and the fifth should match).
12. As intervals expand, the middle note should not have a **"thinner"** tone quality.
13. As intervals expand, reach lower in the body for air.
14. As intervals expand, the lips should remain soft and natural - the corners provide **strength** to support air direction for brass players.
15. Play dissonant intervals with confidence.
16. Breathe on count 4 quarter rests.
17. At the end, play the tritone interval with confidence.

Boldface words are terms that can be found in the glossary at the back of the book.

9–3 Descending Parallel Fifths

Student Goals

1. Breathe together.
2. Start together.
3. Follow through with the same air and **vowel sound**.
4. Release together.
5. **Organize** the end of each note as clearly as the beginning.
6. Strive for a clear tone quality without extraneous noises.
7. The middle note of each group should **match** the surrounding notes in sound and volume.
8. The third note of each group should match the **tonal energy** and **pitch** center of the first note.

9. The wider the interval, the more focused the air stream should be.
10. It is the woodwinds' responsibility to produce accurate intervals to support the brass.
11. As intervals expand, it is important the tonal **resonance** remains consistent from note to note - and instrument to instrument (i.e., the half step and the fifth should match).
12. To achieve proper **balance**, do not let Line A dominate.
13. Breathe on count 4 quarter rests.

9–4 Ascending Parallel Fifths

Student Goals

1. Breathe together.
2. Start together.
3. Follow through with the same air and **vowel sound**.
4. Release together.
5. **Organize** the end of each note as clearly as the beginning.
6. Strive for a clear tone quality without extraneous noises.
7. The middle note of each group should **match** the surrounding notes in sound and volume.
8. The third note of each group should match the **tonal energy** and **pitch** center of the first note.

9. The wider the interval, the more focused the air stream should be.
10. It is the woodwinds' responsibility to produce accurate intervals to support the brass.
11. As intervals expand, it is important the tonal **resonance** remains consistent from note to note – and instrument to instrument (i.e., the half step and the fifth should match).
12. To achieve proper **balance**, do not let Line A dominate.
13. Breathe on count 4 quarter rests.

10. Learning to Play Cadences

10–1 Outlining a Chord Progression With Pedal Tone

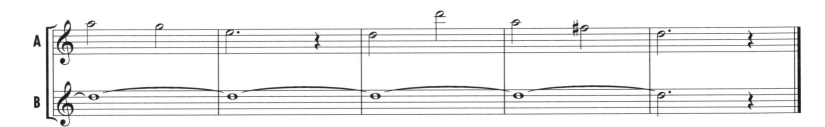

Student Goals for Line A
1. **Match tonal energy**.
2. Keep the volume consistent from note to note.
3. Mentally move your air through the higher note to the note which follows.
4. Every note creates its own interval when played against a **pedal tone**.
5. All intervals should have the same **resonance**.
6. Pay particular attention to the air at the end of each note to connect it smoothly with those that follow.
7. Line A should be played musically with direction and forward motion.
8. Breathe on count 4 quarter rests.
9. Three measure intervals should sound as tonally strong as the two measure interval that begins the exercise.

Student Goals for Line B
1. Breathe together.
2. Start together.
3. Follow through with the same air and **vowel sound**.
4. Release together.
5. **Organize** the end of each note as clearly as the beginning.
6. Vibrato-producing instruments can alternately play a straight tone or with vibrato.
7. Take a breath before one is needed, then re-enter discreetly with the same volume and tonal resonance.

Boldface words are terms that can be found in the glossary at the back of the book.

11. Learning Even Note-Valued Technique

11–1

11–2

11–3

11–4

11–5

11–6

11–7

11–8

11–9

11–10

11–11

11–12

11–13

11–14

11–15

11–16

11–17

11–18

11–19

11–20

Glossary: Concepts, Terms and Techniques

Back of the Note The process of preventing air from decaying before a note is finished. By mentally placing air to the back of a note, the note has a better chance of staying resonant throughout its length.

Back to Front/Front to Back Energy Individuals or sections matching all aspects of wind playing with those performers seated behind them.

Balance (Balanced) Each instrument being heard at the tonal strength appropriate for the music. It is achieved when the conductor has assigned and prioritized the listening responsibilities. Without this information an ensemble will have a difficult time balancing.

Body of Sound The "core" between the articulated front and organized end of each note.

"Bumps" moving from note to note A phenomenon where air at the end of the note slows down, then surges at the beginning of the next note.

Capsule Any module of musical ideas–rhythmic, intervallic, stylistic, etc.

Characteristic Sounds Allowing the instrument to vibrate in the center of the harmonic series. It is a result of the engineering used to create the instruments. Every instrument will produce a characteristic sound if the balance of air, resistance of the instrument, strength of the embouchure and focus of the mind are in balance. If the body interferes with the air, a characteristic sound cannot be achieved.

Color The most mature, vibrant sound, consistent throughout all registers. Specific characteristic sounds combine to create the color of the ensemble. The conductor can create any color desired by layering the characteristic sounds of the instruments in any order.

Color Group Instruments whose characteristic sounds are similar in timbre.

Energy (Energize) A conceptual word relating to ensemble fundamentals. It can describe any aspect of musical performance (i.e., tonal resonance, line movement, specific styles, etc.) The conductor should be very specific in its use.

Ensemble Breathing The action of breathing together.

Firm Articulation A technique where the tongue shape is rounder, and touches the teeth (or reed) harder. The air becomes denser, creating the desired effect without overblowing the harmonic.

Fit Into An instrument, or group of instruments, allowing the timbre of another instrument to dominate the texture.

Focus of Articulation Directing the air behind the tongue to the center of the mouthpiece, creating a stronger front to a note, or series of notes.

Focus of Sound Balancing the air and resistance, allowing the tone quality to vibrate sympathetically within the harmonic series.

Harmonic Series The basis of all musical performance. It controls the quality of all tonal aspects of music. The performer must resonate sympathetically within the series to create an acceptable sound.

Internalized (Internalizing) The technique of a player feeling the pulse within their body. The metronome enables the player to respond aurally; the baton enables the player to respond visually; and the internalized pulse helps the student to respond physically to the movement of the phrase.

Matching (Match) Relating any aspect of playing to a specific player or section. It is a word of reference. Awareness of the conductor's desires is the key to the understanding of matching. For ensemble members to master this skill, the conductor must be very specific.

Model The performer selected by the conductor to demonstrate an aspect of a musical idea. Occasionally an entire section can be utilized the same manner.

Musical Silence A term indicating that the student's mind stays active in the music during times when they aren't actually playing. This keeps the student involved even though they are silent.

Open-throat Release The most resonant organization ending each note. The air is very deep in the body, not allowing the throat to close, or any part of the mouth to move when the sound ends. The embouchure must be perfectly still when the note is released.

Organize (Organized, Organizing) To make the ends of notes as clean and resonant as the beginnings.

Pedal Tone Any note sustained as other notes are moving. Ensembles should learn the skill of staggered-breathing to successfully create the proper function and desired effect of a pedal tone.

Pitch The actual center of sound. It can be used to describe the relationship of one note to another, one performer to another, or one section to another. However, in each instance, it is best to use the word "pitch" for only one definition. For example, only use the word "pitch" when referring to the relationship of one tone to another. Do not confuse your students by using the word "pitch" for multiple concepts.

Resonance (Resonant, Resonate) The quality beyond the core of the sound. It is the result of sympathetic vibrations within the harmonic series. Each performer should be aware of, and sensitive to, the balance of air and resistance that creates their most resonant sound. When individual performers play with resonance, the ensemble inherits a resonance of its own. There is a direct correlation between individual and ensemble resonance. Ensemble tonal resonance can only occur when the correct relationship from section to section is achieved. A layering of tonal colors will help create the ensemble tonal resonance.

Side to Side Energy An individual matching all aspects of wind playing with performers on either side.

"Silent Fingering" To silently finger/position the written music while other sections are playing.

Staggered-breathing Alternately taking breaths within a section or group, allowing a note or phrase to seemingly continue uninterrupted. This technique is most often used with extremely long notes or phrases.

Strength The degree to which a note is articulated. It is important to be consistent throughout a chosen style.

Texture The sound created when all lines of music are in balance and treated properly within the intent of the composer.

Thick Sounds The failure of instruments vibrating sympathetically with each other or within the harmonic series. The unsympathetic vibrations prevent tonal clarity.

Thin (Thinner) Sound The effect of the air stream overblowing the embouchure, or the pitch center being too high in the harmonic series.

Timbre The characteristic quality of an instrument when it is allowed to vibrate sympathetically in the harmonic series.

Tone (Tonal) Color The effect of instrument timbres being layered to create a new, more sophisticated sound.

Tonal Energy The core of a characteristic sound at its freest moment. The tonal energy can be that of an individual or a section. For example, a student can be instructed to match the tonal energy of the first chair flute player, or the trombone section can be asked to match the tonal energy of the trumpet section. Tonal energy in no way affects tonal color.

Tonal Purity The effect of a correct embouchure, correct air/resistance, and the instrument being in responsive working order.

Tonal Strength Allowing the instrument to vibrate within the harmonic series, creating the instrument's most powerful sound.

Transparency All instruments being heard in balance all of the time, satisfying the demands of the music.

Uncharacteristic Sounds The effect of the balance of air, resistance of the instrument, strength of the embouchure and focus of the mind are in disarray. No musician should wish to make an uncharacteristic sound on their instrument.

Vibrancy (Vibrant) The freedom with which an instrument, or instruments, creates its own timbre. The instrument should freely vibrate sympathetically within the harmonic series.

Vowel Sounds Shaping the tongue with vowel sound to create the tone quality the performer desires. Brass instruments use various vowel sounds depending on the register required; however, most woodwind instruments use only one vowel sound.